Exploring Florida's Habitats

by Barbara A. Donovan

Harcourt
SCHOOL PUBLISHERS

D1798500

Cover, ©Getty/44125; p.4, ©Fred Bavendam/Minden Pictures; p.5, ©CORBIS; p.6, ©Arco Images/ Alamy; p.7, ©David Hosking/Alamy, p.8 Lynn Stone/Bruce Coleman Inc; p.9 Bruce Coleman Inc./ Alamy; p.10, (b) ©Joachim Messerschmidt/Bruce Coleman Inc.; (tl) ©Florida Images/Alamy; p.11, ©Joe McDonald/CORBIS; p.12, ©Harcourt; p.13 ©Jh Pete Carmichael; p.14 ©Jack Sullivan/Alamy.

Copyright © by Harcourt, Inc.

All rights reserved. No part of this publication may be reproduced or transmitted in any form or by any means, electronic or mechanical, including photocopy, recording, or any information storage and retrieval system, without permission in writing from the publisher.

Requests for permission to make copies of any part of the work should be addressed to School Permissions and Copyrights, Harcourt, Inc., 6277 Sea Harbor Drive, Orlando, Florida 32887–6777. Fax: 407-345-2418.

CALIFORNIA EXCURSIONS is a trademark of Harcourt, Inc. HARCOURT and the Harcourt Logo are trademarks of Harcourt, Inc., registered in the United States of America and/or other jurisdictions.

Printed in China

ISBN 10:   0-15-379139-X
ISBN 13:   978-0-15-379139-0

Ordering Options
ISBN 10:   0-15-378788-0 (English Language Development Concept Readers Collection, Grade 5)
ISBN 13:   978-0-15-378788-1 (English Language Development Concept Readers Collection, Grade 5)
ISBN 10:   0-15-379169-1 (package of 5)
ISBN 13:   978-0-15-379169-7 (package of 5)

If you have received these materials as examination copies free of charge, Harcourt School Publishers retains title to the materials and they may not be resold. Resale of examination copies is strictly prohibited and is illegal.

Possession of this publication in print format does not entitle users to convert this publication, or any portion of it, into electronic format.

2 3 4 5 6 7 8 9 10 0940 17 16 15 14 13 12 11 10 09

Florida is easy to find. Look at a map of the United States. Florida is at the bottom on the right side of the map. Most of Florida is surrounded by water. On Florida's east coast is the Atlantic Ocean. Florida's west coast touches the Gulf of Mexico.

Florida has a lot of water inland, too. Water helps create many of Florida's habitats. These are the places where plants and animals live. In this book, we will explore five Florida habitats. We will also find out about some animals that live in each one.

Estuary

An estuary is a place where salt water mixes with freshwater. Not all animals can live here. Some animals can only live in salt water. Others can only live in freshwater. Animals had to adapt, or change, to live in an estuary. The water here is not as salty as ocean or gulf water. It also has more salt than freshwater does.

One famous Florida animal lives here. It is the manatee. This huge animal is very gentle. It also helps the environment. Manatees only eat plants. They eat sea grasses and other plants that grow in estuaries. Manatees "mow" the plants like you might mow your lawn. Manatees help keep the plants from growing too thick in the narrow canals.

    Manatees are endangered animals. If people are not careful, soon manatees will be gone from the earth. Manatees are in trouble for several reasons. People are building cities near manatee habitats. People are also careless when driving their boats in manatee habitats. People may hit a manatee with their boat without even knowing it. Manatees swim very slowly. Often they stay just below the surface of the water while they eat plants. Manatees are not fast enough to swim away when boats come near.

Mangrove Forest

We find the mangrove forest farther inland. Mangroves are trees that can live in estuaries. These trees can make the freshwater they need from the salty water there. That's unusual. It's not something all plants can do.

Three kinds of mangrove trees live in this forest. The red mangrove is the most common. This tree can live very close to the salt water. You can see its many roots in the air. They look like a big tent under the tree. These roots help many animals. Small animals hide in the roots to keep away from predators that might eat them.

One animal that lives in the mangrove forest is the American crocodile. It is endangered, too. The crocodile's body can get rid of the salt in salty water. This crocodile is a very dangerous animal. It likes living in isolated places. It's never a good idea to bother a crocodile. A crocodile will chase and fight any person or animal that disturbs it.

Other dangerous animals live in the mangroves, too. One is the cottonmouth snake. This snake eats other animals. The cottonmouth has two very long teeth called fangs. They have poison in them. The snake uses its fangs to catch its dinner.

Coastal Prairie

The earth is dry on the coastal prairie. This land is between two other kinds of land. The low mud flats of the ocean are on one side. High and dry land is on the other side. Most plants and animals cannot live in the coastal prairie. There is not enough freshwater for them to survive.

The coastal prairie is a good habitat for some snakes. One snake that lives here is the eastern diamondback snake. This snake is a kind of rattlesnake. It rattles the end of its tail to warn people and animals that it will bite. Its bite is poisonous.

Another kind of snake found in the coastal prairie is the scarlet king snake. This snake is not a poisonous snake. However, it looks like the coral snake, which has a poisonous bite. Animals that might otherwise try to eat the scarlet king snake leave it alone. They think that if they try to eat this snake, they will be bitten and poisoned. Looking like the coral snake may often save the life of the scarlet king snake.

Hardwood Hammock

Next we'll explore a hardwood hammock. To you, a hammock might mean a piece of cloth that you hang between two trees. You might lie in this kind of hammock to rest in the shade. A hardwood hammock is a place where many hardwood trees live close together. These trees have wood that is very hard. The red maple and mahogany are two kinds of trees that live here. The hammock is similar to a small island. The land here is only a few inches above water. Freshwater surrounds it.

One animal that lives here is the Florida box turtle. This animal has a high shell. It looks similar to a box. This turtle can almost completely hide itself in

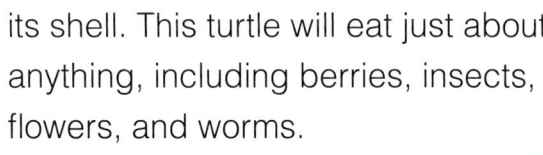 its shell. This turtle will eat just about anything, including berries, insects, flowers, and worms.

Another animal that lives here is the opossum. This animal spends much of its time in the trees. It, too, eats just about anything. Some bigger animals try to eat opossums. An opossum has a good trick to fool bigger animals. The opossum will lie still and "play dead" until the big animal leaves. Then the opossum will get up and go on its way.

Pinelands

Our last place to explore is the pinelands. As you might guess, many pine trees grow here. The land is high and very dry. Much of the land is a type of rock called limestone. It has many tiny holes in it. Seeds from pine trees drop into the holes. Some holes might have soil in them. The seeds in those holes might grow into trees.

You can find two different kinds of big cats living here. One is easier to find. It is the bobcat. A bobcat eats meat. This cat may walk as far as fifty miles (80.48 km) in one day in search of animals to eat.

The other cat that lives here is very hard to find. It's the Florida panther. This is an endangered animal that is close to extinction. There are fewer than eighty of them living today. The panther is in the same family as the mountain lion.

People are working hard to save the Florida panther. This big cat used to be the king of the pinelands before people hunted it. People also have taken over the panther habitat. Today this animal is in great danger.

Florida is a land with many different habitats. Most of the land here is low. It's also near water. Plants and animals might live under the water in an estuary. They also might live in the trees of a mangrove forest. Plants and animals might live in a dry place near the water in a coastal prairie. They might live in a hardwood hammock with water all around them. They might even live on high ground in the pinelands. If you explore Florida, you can find animals and plants that have learned to live in many different kinds of places.

Scaffolded Language Development

CONNOTATION AND DENOTATION Write the following words and phrases from the book on the board:

careless	poisonous snake
dangerous animal	pinelands
trouble	nest

Review the definition of each word or phrase with students. Tell them that the definition of a word is called its "denotation." The part of a word's meaning that is implied is called it's "connotation." Suggest to students that words can have either a positive or a negative connotation. Discuss the connotation of each word or phrase on the board.

Have students make a two-column chart with the heads *Positive* and *Negative* and sort the following words and phrases by their connotation.

box turtle	coral snake
predator	endangered
fresh water	bite

 Science

Habitat Poster Ask pairs of students to summarize what they learned about one of Florida's animal habitats on a poster.

School-Home Connection

Discuss Florida Have students share some of the things they learned in this book about Florida with family members. Have them talk about how these places compare with where you live.

Word Count: 1,189 (with graphic 1,195)